Orang–utans in Danger

by Helen Orme

CONTENTS

Words that appear **in bold** are explained in the glossary.

Copyright © **ticktock Entertainment Ltd** 2008
First published in Great Britain in 2008 by **ticktock Media Ltd.**,
Unit 2, Orchard Business Centre, North Farm Road,
Tunbridge Wells, Kent, TN2 3XF
ISBN 978 1 84696 780 1 pbk
Printed in China

We would like to thank Penny Worms, the National Literacy Trust, and our consultant Dr. Gary Shapiro Ph.D.,
Vice President, Orangutan Foundation International

Picture credits: t=top, b=bottom, c=centre, l-left, r=right
Alamy: 12-13, 15, 16-17, 24-25. Corbis: 10-11, 22-23, 25t. Digital Vision: OFC, 4-5, 8, 9, 10-11, 14, 22-23, 24, 25bl, 26, 27, 28,
31, 32. FLPA: 7c, 25br. Orangutan Foundation UK: 29.
Every effort has been made to trace the copyright holders, and we apologise in advance for any unintentional omissions. We would
be pleased to insert the appropriate acknowledgements in any subsequent edition of this publication.

THE WORLD OF THE ORANG-UTAN

Orang-utans are large tree-living **apes**. They live in **rainforests** on the islands of Sumatra and Borneo in South-east Asia.

Female orang-utans usually have just one baby at a time.

Baby orang-utans have a lot to learn. For the first seven years of their life, their mothers will teach them all they need to know about living in the rainforest.

WHERE THEY LIVE

The orang-utans' rainforests are being destroyed. Now they only live in the red areas shown on the main map.

PACIFIC OCEAN

SOUTH-EAST ASIA

MALAYSIA

SUMATRA

BORNEO

INDONESIA

ADULT ORANG-UTANS

Adult orang-utans live alone. Each orang-utan has its own **territory** *in the rainforest.*

Males and females only meet for mating.

Male orang-utans often fight if another male comes near.

Male orang-utans are nearly twice as big as females. They have large cheek pouches at the sides of their faces.

FOREST GIANTS

A big male orang-utan's
arms can span 2.3 metres.

THE HUNT FOR FOOD

Orang-utans need to travel long distances through the rainforest to find their food.

They mostly travel above the ground, using their powerful arms to swing from one branch to another.

Orang-utans eat many different sorts of food, such as fruit and leaves, birds' eggs, snails and **termites**.

BABY FOOD FACT

For the first few months, baby orang-utans only drink their mothers' milk. Later, they eat fruit which is chewed and softened for them by their mothers.

NIGHT IN THE FOREST

At night the rainforest is full of the sounds of insects and **nocturnal** creatures, such as lorises.

Orang-utans build sleeping nests high up in the forks of trees.

These nests are made by bending branches into a bowl shape. The orang-utans fill the bowls with leaves to make them soft and snug.

Lorises are small, tree-living animals with thick fur.

RAINFOREST IN DANGER

The biggest threat facing the orang-utan is the destruction of the rainforest.

The islands where orang-utans live are crowded with people. Many people are poor. Cutting timber from the forest is often the only way they can earn enough to live.

In some places there are laws to protect the forest. But without enough people to enforce the laws, the **logging** is not stopped.

WHY ARE THE TREES CUT DOWN?

- Rainforest trees are cut down for timber or to be made into paper.

- Gold has been found in the rainforest. Trees are cut down to make room for gold mines.

- People need farmland to grow food.

POACHERS

Some people kill or capture orang-utans.
This is called poaching.

In the past, some orang-utans were killed for food.
Now the poaching problem has become much worse
because many people want baby orang-utans for pets.

The poachers treat the orang-utans very cruelly.
Often the mother is killed to make it easier to take
the baby.

Many baby orang-utans die before they reach their
new owners.

ORANG-UTANS FOR SALE

Baby orang-utans can be sold for a lot of money. But this does not mean that they are well looked after by the poachers.

They are often put into tiny cages and sold at markets by the side of the road. Sometimes they are not fed properly.

RESCUE CENTRES

Orang-utans do not make good pets. When they become adults, they are very strong and can be bad tempered.

When people get tired of their pet orang-utans, many of the animals are killed.

The lucky ones might go to a rescue centre. Here they are looked after until they are ready to live by themselves, back in the rainforest.

At rescue centres vets check the orang-utans to make sure they have not picked up a disease while they have been living with humans.

TEACHING ORANG-UTANS TO BE WILD

In the wild, young orang-utans learn what food is safe to eat, and where to find it. They also learn how to travel through the rainforest and how to stay safe.

Babies that have been kept as pets do not know how to do these things.

The rescue centre carers start to teach the babies by putting food on feeding platforms up in the rainforest trees.

Slowly, the young orang-utans will learn where to find their own food.

PROTECTING THE ORANG-UTANS

*The rescued orang-utans are released into **nature reserves**.*

Forest rangers patrol the reserves. Loggers and poachers are kept out.

But there are still problems. Governments of the countries where orang-utans live cannot afford to pay for enough rangers to make sure that the animals are safe.

Outside the reserves, orang-utans are not protected at all. Their **habitat** is disappearing fast.

EXTINCTION

There are probably only 25,000 orang-utans left in the wild. Ten years ago there were twice as many. Unless more is done to protect them, scientists say that orang-utans could become **extinct** in the wild in just ten years.

GLOSSARY

extinct When a type of animal or plant completely disappears.

forest rangers People whose job it is to look after protected nature reserves and the animals that live there.

habitat Somewhere that suits a particular wild animal or plant.

logging Cutting down trees for wood.

nature reserves Protected areas where the killing of animals or the cutting down of trees is against the law.

nocturnal When an animal is only active at night.

rainforests Warm, wet forests, often found near the Equator, where there are many types of plants and animals.

termites Insects a bit like ants that live in large groups.

territory The area in which an animal or animal family lives.

INDEX